The Robotx
Get Help from Simple Machines

Winding Around

The Screw

Written by Gerry Bailey   Illustrated by Mike Spoor

Get Help from Simple Machines

Crabtree Publishing Company
www.crabtreebooks.com
1-800-387-7650

PMB 59051, 350 Fifth Ave.
59ₜₕ Floor,
New York, NY 10118

616 Welland Ave.
St. Catharines, ON
L2M 5V6

Published by Crabtree Publishing in 2014

Author: Gerry Bailey
Illustrator: Mike Spoor
Editor: Kathy Middleton
Proofreader: Crystal Sikkens
End matter: Kylie Korneluk
Production coordinator and
   Prepress technician: Ken Wright
Print coordinator: Margaret Amy Salter

Copyright © 2013
BrambleKids Ltd.

Photographs:
All images are Shutterstock.com unless otherwise stated.
Pg 9 – (t) MarFot (b)
Pg 11 – Parys Ryszard
Pg 12/13 - PRESNIAKOV OLEKSANDR
Pg 13 - Przemek Tokar
Pg 16/17 – Alamy
Pg 20 – Thomas Oswald
Pg 23 – (t) MarFot (c) zcool (b) Wikipedia
Pg 24 – (t) Coprid (b) Givaga
Pg 25 – In Green

Printed in Canada/022014/MA20131220

Library and Archives Canada Cataloguing in Publication

Bailey, Gerry, author
    Winding around : the screw / written by Gerry Bailey ; illustrated by Mike Spoor.

(The robotx get help from simple machines)
Includes index.
Issued in print and electronic formats.
ISBN 978-0-7787-0421-8 (bound).--ISBN 978-0-7787-0427-0 (pbk.).--
ISBN 978-1-4271-7539-7 (pdf).--ISBN 978-1-4271-7533-5 (html)

    1. Screws--Juvenile literature. I. Spoor, Mike, illustrator II. Title.

TJ1338.B35 2014   j621.8'82   C2013-908719-2
                               C2013-908720-6

Library of Congress Cataloging-in-Publication Data

Bailey, Gerry, author.
 Winding around : the screw / written by Gerry Bailey ; illustrated by Mike Spoor.
   pages cm. -- (The Robotx get help from simple machines)
 Audience: Ages 5-8.
 Audience: K to grade 3.
 Includes index.
 ISBN 978-0-7787-0421-8 (reinforced library binding) -- ISBN 978-0-7787-0427-0 (pbk.) -- ISBN 978-1-4271-7539-7 (electronic pdf) -- ISBN 978-1-4271-7533-5 (electronic html)
 1. Screws--Juvenile literature. 2. Simple machines--Juvenile literature. I. Spoor, Mike, illustrator. II. Title. III. Title: Screw.

TJ1338.B25 2014
621.8'11--dc23
                           2013050835

Contents

The Robotx

Meet   RobbO   and   RobbEE

The robots' workshop

RobbO and RobbEE are putting together a new machine in their workshop.

It has arrived in lots and lots of pieces.

A machine is...

A machine is a tool used to make work easier. Work is the effort needed to create force. A force is a push or pull on an object. Machines allow us to push, pull, or lift a heavy weight much easier, or using less effort. All machines are made up of at least one **simple machine**.

There are six kinds of simple machines. Some have just one part that moves. Others are made up of two or more parts. The six simple machines are:

- **lever**
- **wedge**
- **pulley**
- **screw**
- **inclined plane**
- **wheel and axle**

In this book, the Robotx will help us learn all about the screw.

The two robots look through the pieces scattered all over the workshop floor.

"This goes here," says RobbO.
"And that goes there,"
adds RobbEE.
"But how are they held together?"

The answer
is screws.

RobbO finds the box of screws. Right away they can see how things are joined together.

RobbO takes the screwdriver and
fits the tip into the slot on the
head, or top, of the screw.
He turns the screwdriver, and
the screw begins to slowly
wind its way into
the metal piece.

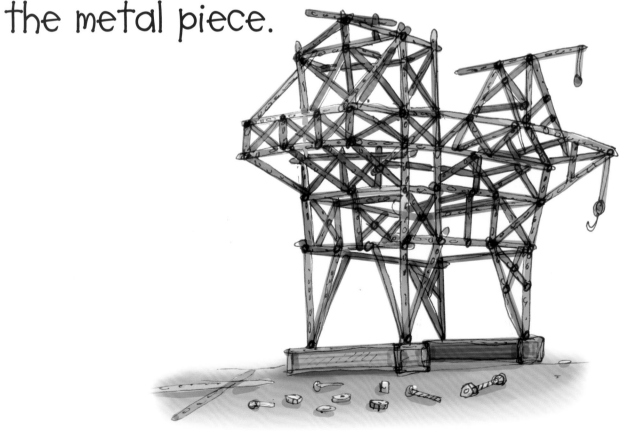

Turning the screw

A screwdriver is a device used to turn a screw. Its tip fits into the slot in the head of the screw. The user twists the handle to create a turning force. This turns the spiral ridge around the screw a long way, but moves the screw as a whole only a short distance.

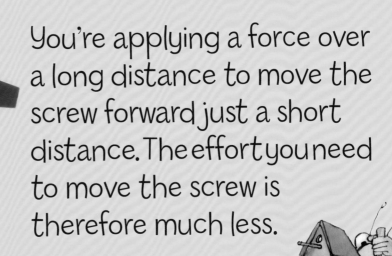

You're applying a force over a long distance to move the screw forward just a short distance. The effort you need to move the screw is therefore much less.

A power drill drives a screw-shaped bit, or cutting piece, in the same way. Less force is needed to make a hole with a power drill.

A screw

A screw is a simple machine made up of two parts. A raised **ridge** wraps around a cylinder or rod in one long spiral. The raised ridge is the main part of the screw.

The ridge is called the thread. The thread acts just like a ramp, or inclined plane.

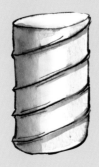

Because the screw has threads, it takes longer to turn a screw than to hammer a nail. However, a screw takes less effort and makes the job easier.

An augur is a very large screw used as a drill. It can bore, or cut, a hole into the ground.

Through rock

RobbO and RobbEE are exploring in a tunnel where a huge drill is being used. The Robotx want to see how the giant drill works.

The huge, screw-shaped drill bores a hole into the rock by spinning. Drills like these are used to dig for coal or to make tunnels for vehicles.

Another screw inside the machine carries the rock or coal out through the arm and onto a **conveyor belt** to be taken out of the mine.

Mining drill bits

12

Archimedes' screw

"Let's have lunch," says RobbO, "and I'll tell you a story about another kind of screw."

Over two thousand years ago in the city of Syracuse, when it was still part of Greece, there lived a great scientist and **mathematician** named Archimedes. Knowing how clever he was, the king asked Archimedes to design a great ship. The king wanted the ship to be able to carry 600 people and contain a garden, a gymnasium, and a **temple**.

Archimedes knew that a ship this big would take in a lot of water through its hull, or body. So, he invented a machine that would get rid of the unwanted water.

His machine was made up of a screw inside a cylinder, or tube. The screw could be turned by hand. The bottom of the tube was placed into the water inside the bottom of the ship. As the screw was turned, the water was lifted up through the tube and outside the ship.

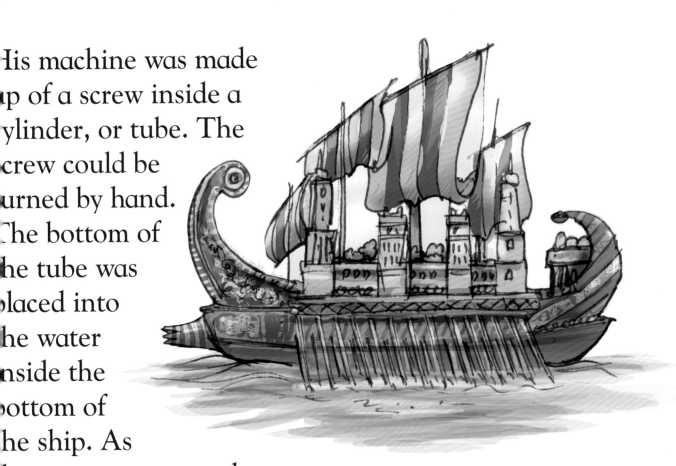

Since then, Archimedes' screws have been used to lift water from rivers into **irrigation** ditches. These ditches carry water to fields that are far away from the river.

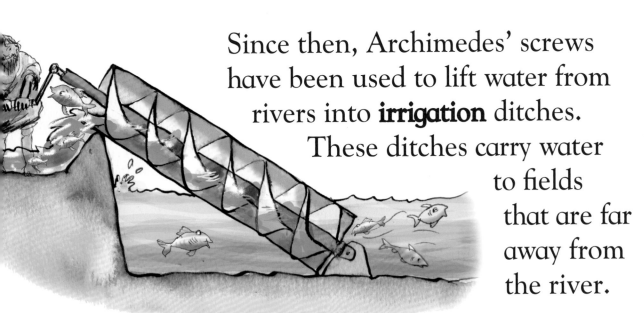

Screws that lift

RobbEE knows where there is a really fun Archimedes' screw. It's at the water park. This screw raises water up to the top of a waterslide ramp to keep it wet and slippery for the ride down.

"Wow!" cries RobbEE, as they race down the slope.

This ride at an amusement park in California uses an Archimedes' screw.

The swivel chair

RobbO looks at RobbEE's chair. "Would you like to sit a bit higher?" he asks. "Your chair is a kind of screw. I just need to swing you around, and the chair will go up." RobbO twirls RobbEE around.

"That was easy!" exclaims RobbEE.

"Yes," says RobbO. "It was the screw that did the work. It had to travel a long way around to raise you up just a short distance."

"But it would have taken a lot more effort to lift you up on my own!"

Screws that press

Screws were first used to change a force that goes around and around to a force that goes up and down.

Cider press

A cider press squeezes the juice from apples. It is made up of a large screw that moves a plate up and down. A handle at the end of the screw is used to turn the press. As the screw turns, it moves the plate which presses down onto the fruit to squeeze out the juice.

Printing press

The first printing presses worked like the cider press. A screw system was used to press a piece of paper down onto a square of blocks covered with ink. Each block had a letter on it, and these were arranged into words.

Corkscrew

A corkscrew winds into a cork and makes it easier to pull it out of the bottle neck.

Flower press

A screw press can put a lot of pressure on something, such as a flower, to make it flat. The screws have little wings that make turning easier.

Screws that grip

The robots are
rock-climbing.
They attach their
climbing ropes to
a special clamp
called a maillon.
It is a metal loop
in the shape of
the letter C.
It opens and
closes tight
using a screw.

Screwed in

C-clamp

A C-clamp uses a screw device to hold something in place. Turning the handle of the screw creates a huge amount of downward pressure. The pressure holds an object firmly between the end of the screw and one end of the C.

Light bulb

The bottom of a light bulb is a screw. The light bulb screws into the light socket on the ceiling or in a lamp.

Jar lid

The inside of a jar lid is made like a screw so that the lid can hold the jar closed.

The screws that RobbO used to put his new machine together were pointed at the tip. But there is another kind of screw, too. It has a flat end and is called a bolt.

Nuts and bolts

A bolt is a screw with a flat end. A bolt is used with a nut.

bolt

nut

A nut is a six-sided ring that screws onto the bolt.

To tighten it, you can use a wrench that fits onto the head of the bolt or the nut. The wrench acts like a lever to apply a strong turning force to the gripped bolt or nut.

The car jack

RobbO needs to change a tire on his car. But he'll have to lift the car first to get the old wheel off.

Fortunately, he has a useful kind of screw handy that will do the job for him. It's called a jack.

The jack has a screw inside. When RobbO turns the handle, it turns the screw that raises the arms of the jack. This lifts the car.

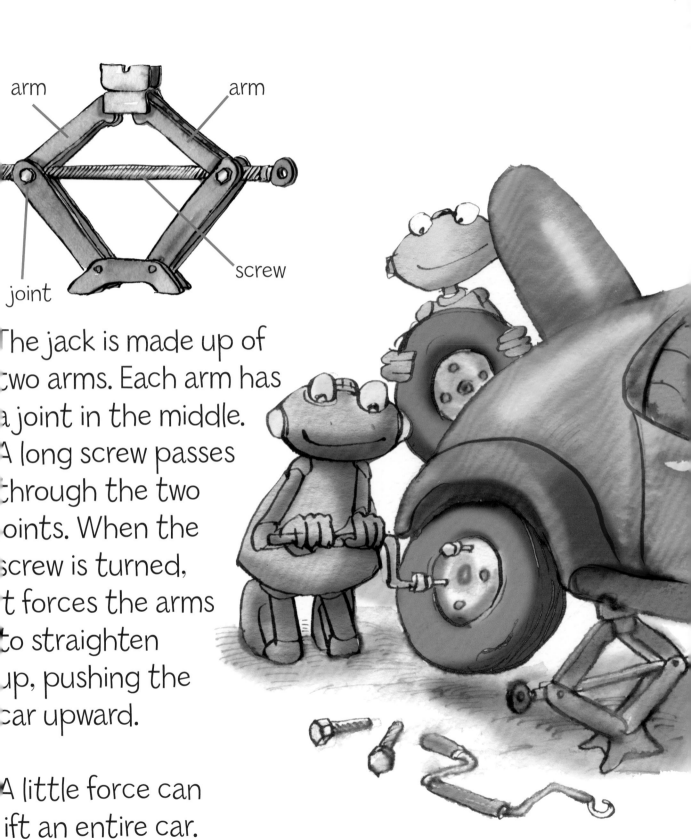

arm

arm

screw

joint

The jack is made up of two arms. Each arm has a joint in the middle. A long screw passes through the two joints. When the screw is turned, it forces the arms to straighten up, pushing the car upward.

A little force can lift an entire car.

Robbo's science workshop

All the robots are at the workshop to learn about the screw.

A screw is a simple machine. It's shaped like a cylinder, but instead of smooth sides, it has a raised ridge that forms a spiral around it from top to bottom.

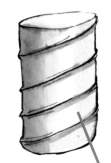

thread

The ridge around the screw is called a thread. As the thread turns, it cuts into material and slowly draws the screw into it.

ramp

A screw acts like a kind of ramp, or inclined plane. In fact, a screw is a ramp in disguise.

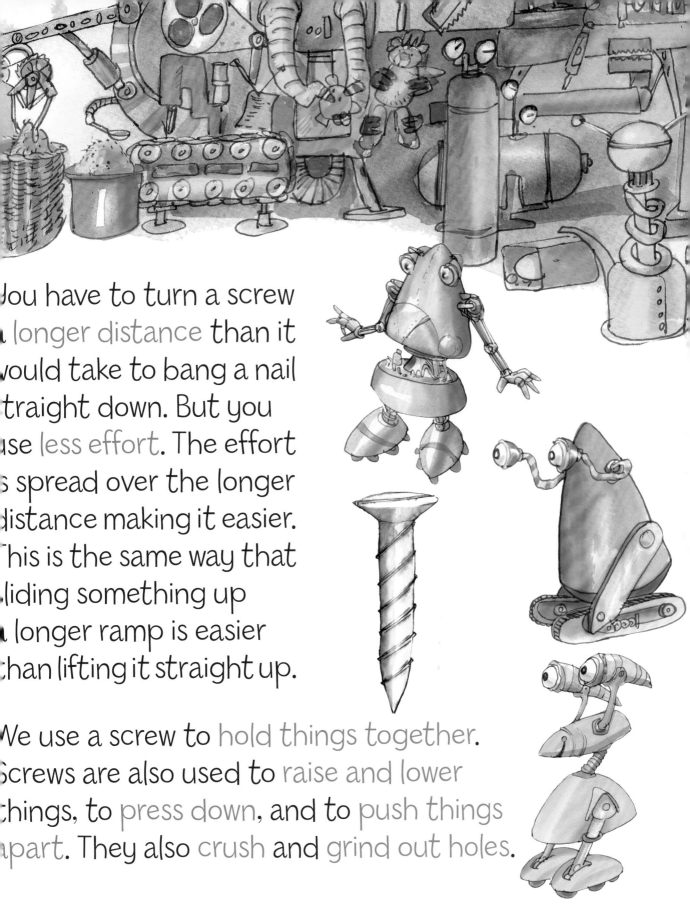

You have to turn a screw a longer distance than it would take to bang a nail straight down. But you use less effort. The effort is spread over the longer distance making it easier. This is the same way that sliding something up a longer ramp is easier than lifting it straight up.

We use a screw to hold things together. Screws are also used to raise and lower things, to press down, and to push things apart. They also crush and grind out holes.

A helicopter machine

The Robotx have built a wonderful machine using a screw. When the screw turns, it will make the machine spiral up into the air.

Airplane **propellers**, helicopter blades, and ship propellers all work the same way as a screw. They move something forward through air or water.

Learning more

Books

Put Screws to the Test
By Roseann Feldmann and Sally M. Walker
(Lerner Publishing, 2011)

How Toys Work: Screws, Nuts, and Bolts
By Sian Smith
(Heinemann, 2012)

Get to Know: Screws
By Jennifer Christiansen
(Crabtree Publishing, 2009)

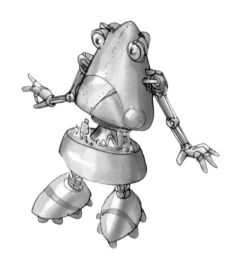

Websites

www.ehow.com/how-does_4600493_a-screw-work.html
Examples of how screws work and how to use them.

www.mocomi.com/screw
An animated video on screws and a short description on
how they work.

www.edheads.org/activities/simple-machines/
An educational activity on screws and other
simple machines.

Glossary

conveyor belt A belt or chain on rollers used to carry things

inclined plane A slanted surface connecting a lower point to a higher point

irrigation The process of moving water to dry land to help with growing crops

lever A bar that rests on a support called a fulcrum which lifts or moves loads

mathematician Someone who is good at math

merchant A person who sells things

propellers A type of fan that creates power by rotating

pulley A simple machine that uses grooved wheels and a rope to raise, lower, or move a load

ridge A raised, spiral edge around the screw

screw An inclined plane wrapped around a pole which holds things together or lifts materials

simple machine A machine that makes work easier by transferring force from one point to another

temple A holy place; usually religious

wedge Two inclined planes joined together used to split things

wheel and axle A wheel with a rod, called an axle, through its center which lifts or moves loads

Index